FRED'S ROUND THE WORLD COOK BOOK

Recipes by Jackie Burrow

Illustrated by Charlie Starkey

RULES OF THE KITCHEN

Always wash your hands before you start to cook.
Wear an apron to protect you and your clothes.
Read the recipe right through before you start
and make sure you have all the necessary ingredients
and tools before you start.
If you have to use sharp knives, ask an adult
to help you.
Ask an adult to help you to light the oven or grill
and always check you have turned them off when you
have finished cooking.
Always keep handles of saucepans turned towards the
middle of the cooker so they can't be knocked over.
Always use thick oven gloves (**not** a tea towel) for
taking things out of the oven. If the dish is large
and heavy or contains hot fat, ask an adult to
take it out for you.
Always mop up anything you drop on the floor
immediately to prevent an accident.
Never leave food to cook without someone watching it –
do not do something else at the same time.
If you do burn or cut yourself, put it under cold
water at once, and call an adult to give you first aid.

Before we prepare for take off, it is essential to read the rules!

A Carousel Book
Transworld Publishers Ltd.

In the recipes the temperatures are marked like this: **200°C (400°F), Gas Mark 6.**

C is for the Celsius Centigrade, **F** for the Fahrenheit temperature and **Gas Mark** for the number on a gas oven.

Ask an adult to show you which method your oven uses.

Here is a temperature equivalents chart:

Oven temperature chart

°C	°F	Gas Mark	Description
110	225	$\frac{1}{4}$	Very cool
120	250	$\frac{1}{2}$	Very cool
140	275	1	Cool
150	300	2	Cool
160	325	3	Moderate
180	350	4	Moderate
190	375	5	Moderately hot
200	400	6	Moderately hot
220	425	7	Hot
230	450	8	Hot
240	475	9	Very hot

And if you are puzzled by any of the cookery terms you find in the recipes, look them up on the list on page 32.

Here is the route we shall be taking, and the delectable dishes we hope to sample along the way are listed, too.

Why is the balloon called *Flour Power*?

Because it doesn't have an engine – it's self-raising!

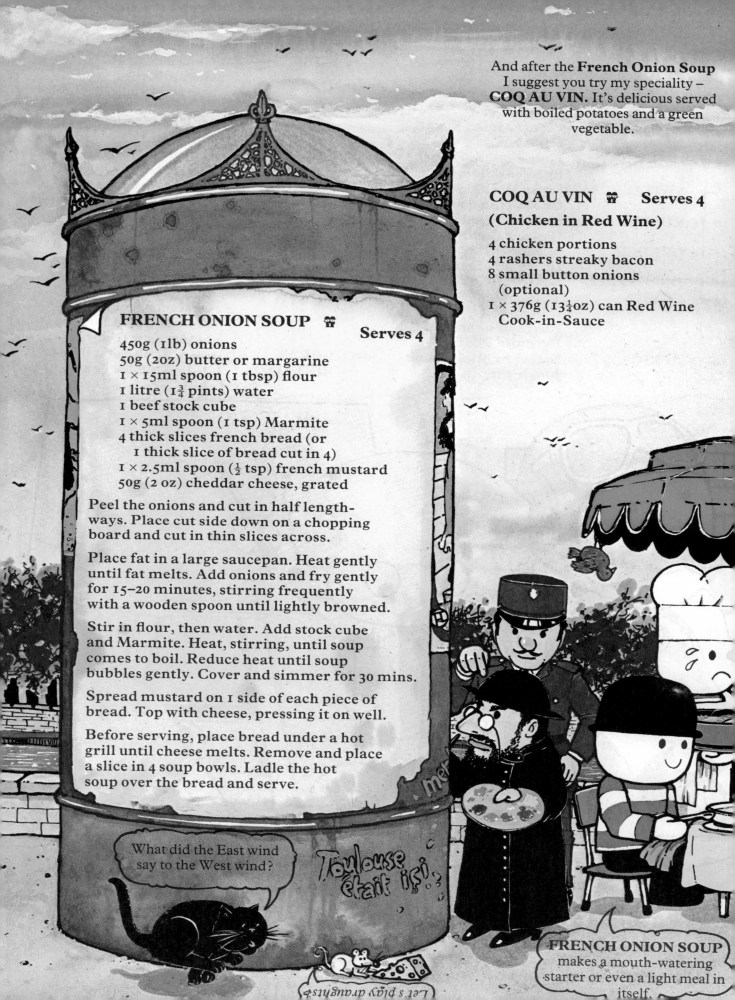

And this is what you do:

Set oven at 190°C (375°F), Gas Mark 5.

Wash and dry the chicken portions and place in a casserole dish.

Cut off bacon rind with scissors. Cut each rasher in half then roll up. Place bacon rolls on top of the chicken.

Peel the onions and add them whole to the casserole. Pour over the can of Red Wine sauce.

Cover casserole and bake in a pre-heated oven for 1½ hours.

FOUR SEASONS PIZZA, 🍕

tastes just as good, hot or cold.

I've laid out all the ingredients on the table below.

This is how you make the dough base:
First of all, set your oven at 200°C (400°F), Gas Mark 6.
Put flour and salt in a mixing bowl.
Cut fat into bits. Add to flour and rub in with fingertips until mixture resembles fine breadcrumbs.
Stir in milk with a round-bladed knife to make a soft dough.

Use hands to place dough on a lightly floured surface and **knead** gently to give a smooth ball of dough. Use a rolling pin to roll out the dough to a 25cm (10 inch) round.

Grease a baking sheet. To make the dough easier to lift, fold it into 4, lift onto the sheet then unfold again.

SCONE DOUGH

225g (8oz) self-raising flour

50g (2oz) butter or margarine

I pinch of salt

150ml (¼ pint) milk

PIZZA TOPPING

225g (8oz) onions

2 × 15ml spoons (tbsp) cooking oil

I × 15ml spoon (1tbsp) tomato puree

I × 2.5ml spoon (½ tsp) dried oregano or mixed herbs

50g (2oz) cooked ham

50g (2oz) streaky bacon

50g (2oz) button mushrooms

I large tomato

50g (2oz) processed cheddar cheese slice

4 anchovy fillets (optional)

When the dough base is ready – here's how to make the topping:

Peel and slice onions as for the **French onion soup, p. 4.** Pour the oil into a medium-sized saucepan. Add onions and cover. Cook over a gentle heat for 15 minutes until soft.

Spread tomato puree over dough. Sprinkle with herbs. Spread cooked onions evenly over pizza.

Mark pizza into 4 quarters. Chop ham into small squares and put on one quarter. Cut off bacon rind with scissors and snip bacon into pieces for another quarter. Slice mushrooms thinly for another and brush lightly with oil. Slice tomato for the last quarter. Cut each cheese slice in 4 and place over centre of pizza. Put an anchovy strip down each quarter.

Bake in a pre-heated oven for 20 mins.

Serves 4

Look at Italy's famous Tower of Pisa – it was built over 600 years ago. I wonder what makes it lean?

A very strict diet!

Never leave anything cooking unwatched – the food could be burned and spoilt – and it may even cause a dangerous fire.

SPAGHETTI BOLOGNESE

MENU

Serves 4

450g (1lb) lean minced beef
1 × 376g (13¼oz) can Tomato and Onion Cook-in-Sauce
1 × 2.5ml spoon (½ tsp) dried herbs (optional)
2 litres (3½ pints) water
1 × 5ml spoon (1 tsp) salt
1 × 15ml spoon (1 tbsp) cooking oil
225g (8oz) spaghetti
25g (1oz) grated parmesan cheese

Put the minced beef in a medium-sized saucepan. Pour in the tomato and onion sauce. Add herbs and stir until well mixed.

Heat gently, stirring with a wooden spoon until mixture boils. Immediately reduce the heat until there are just small bubbles on the top. Cover and simmer gently for 30 minutes. Stir now and then to prevent mixture sticking.

Meanwhile, pour water into large saucepan and add salt and oil. Bring water to boil.

Hold the spaghetti in a bundle at one end. Lower the other end of the spaghetti into the boiling water. In a few seconds it will soften and you'll be able to coil the rest of the spaghetti into the water. **Be careful to keep your hands well away from the boiling water – use a long wooden spoon to help the last ends in.** Boil gently for 10–15 minutes until cooked.

Drain spaghetti and arrange on a serving dish. Put Bolognese sauce in the centre and sprinkle cheese on top. **Serve hot.**

I'm a Chow who's enjoying this chow!

I can't find my way through the maze. Can you?

Spaghetti is at its best when soft but still slightly chewy or *Al Dente* as the Italians say.

Here we are in Switzerland, and as grass is a bit sparse on the mountain tops, the rabbits are making **CHOCOLATE SNOWBALLS,**

For 6 Snowballs you will need:

100g (4oz) cake crumbs
  (e.g. plain sponge or madeira)
50g (2oz) ground almonds
50g (2oz) icing sugar
4 × 15ml spoons (4 tbsp) cocoa powder
50g (2oz) butter
1 × 15ml spoon (1 tbsp) orange juice
25g (1oz) chocolate vermicelli
6 paper bun cases

The rabbits will tell you what to do.

The Alps are Europe's largest mountain range – they cover parts of Austria, France, Germany, Italy, Rumania, Yugoslavia and Switzerland.

1. Mix together the cake crumbs, ground almonds, icing sugar and cocoa powder in a mixing bowl.

2. Cut butter into small bits and rub into the mixture with fingertips until no lumps of butter are left and the mixture is sticky.

3. Stir in orange juice until mixture forms a ball. Divide this into 6 equal pieces and roll each into a ball using palms of hands. Place on a plate and chill in refrigerator for 30 minutes until firm.

4. Spoon vermicelli onto centre of a sheet of greaseproof paper. Roll a ball in vermicelli until covered all over. Lift edges of paper to get vermicelli in centre again and repeat until all 6 balls are coated. Place snowballs in paper cases and chill until needed.

Ballooning round the world is quite a challenge, but if the morning begins with a big bowl of **MUESLI**, that energy-giving Swiss breakfast, we will be riding high for the rest of the day! It's easy to make too –

This is what you need for 4 bowlfuls:

100g (4oz) instant porridge oats
25g (1oz) nuts (e.g. hazelnuts, walnuts, almonds)
25g (1oz) raisins
25g (1oz) sultanas
25g (1oz) brown sugar
25g (1oz) dried apricots (optional)

1 apple
1 banana
150ml (¼ pint) yoghurt

Muesli makes a good cold pudding too. You can eat it with milk or by itself. It's delicious!

Who told you?

A little swallow!

The Muesli is made like this:

Put the porridge oats into a mixing bowl. Roughly chop the nuts (use a mixture or just one type) and add to the bowl. Add raisins, sultanas and sugar. If using apricots, cut into small pieces with scissors into the bowl. Mix all ingredients in the bowl and leave until required. (You can do all this the night before.) Just before serving, cut the apple into quarters and remove cores. Coarsely grate the apple, including its peel, and stir into mixture in the bowl.
Divide between 4 serving bowls. Spoon an equal amount of yoghurt on top of each. Finish with thinly sliced banana.

*The **Chocolate Snowball** mixture can be made into small **truffles** by rolling it into smaller balls and placing them in small sweetcases. They make a lovely present to give at any time.*

*Sounds a good idea – and for an extra special present for your favourite grown-up, substitute the orange juice in the recipe for **brandy** or **rum**.*

The **Moscow State Circus** is one of the most famous circuses in the world. It is the home of the Solokhin Brothers, who hold a World Record for High Wire Walking.

RUSSIAN SALAD ♀

Serve[...]

227g (8oz) pkt. frozen mixed vegetables
225g (8oz) cooked potato **or** 397g (14oz) can potatoes, drained
150ml (¼pt) mayonnaise
1 × 15ml spoon (1tbsp) lemon juic[...]
Salt and pepper 1 small lettuce

Cook frozen veg. according to packet instructions. Drain and leave to cool. Cut potatoes in small cubes. Add to mixed vegetables. Mix mayonnaise with lemon juice. Add salt and pepper. Stir into vegetable mixture. Wash and dry lettuce. Arrange on serving plate. Pile salad in centre. Chill until needed.

1 medium cauliflower

300ml (½ pt) water

Pinch of salt

25g (1oz) butter or margarine

2 × 15ml spoons (2 tbsp) flour

300ml (½ pt) milk

50g (2oz) processed cheddar cheese slices, chopped

50g (2oz) cooked ham, chopped

1 × 5ml spoon (1 tsp) made mustard

Salt and pepper

Par[...] spri[...]

We've landed in Russia and we're in the arena of the famous Moscow State Circus cooking up some **COSSACK CAULIFLOWER**.

With the ingredients on the table I shall have enough for **4 servings** for a light meal or **6 servings** as a vegetable with a main meal.

This is what you do:

Cut off the coarse stalks at the base of the cauliflower so it stands up evenly and wash well.

Pour water into a saucepan just big enough to hold the cauliflower. Add salt. Put in cauliflower and cover.

Heat until water boils, then reduce heat until water bubbles gently. Simmer for about 10 minutes until cauliflower is just tender.

Meanwhile make the sauce: Melt the butter in a saucepan. Stir in flour, then milk. Cook over gentle heat, stirring all the time until sauce thickens and boils. Reduce heat and simmer gently for 1 minute, stirring. Add cheese, ham, mustard, salt and pepper. Stir until cheese melts.

Carefully drain cauliflower and place on a large serving plate. Pour sauce over cauliflower. Garnish (decorate) with parsley sprig. **Serve at once.**

Who was Egg White?

Snow White's brother.

I don't get the yolk.

I'm armless. I wouldn't hurt a fly!

Before you play **GREEK STATUES**, why not make some? They will keep for 2 weeks in a covered container, and make good presents. You'll need:

100g (4oz) ground almonds
50g (2oz) icing sugar, sieved
50g (2oz) caster sugar
1 egg white

If you have never separated egg white from the yolk before ask an adult to show you what to do. It's important that no yolk falls in!

This is how you make the paste:

Mix the ground almonds, icing sugar and caster sugar in a mixing bowl.

Whisk the egg white in another bowl until frothy but not stiff.

Add most of the egg white to the sugary mixture and stir to a firm, doughy paste. If paste is too thick and dry, add remaining egg white. If too sticky to handle, add a few spoons of sieved icing sugar. Sprinkle working surface with a little sieved icing sugar. Knead paste gently until smooth.

And this is how you make the statues:

Pull off a small piece of paste and roll between your palms to form a ball or sausage. Mould this into any shape you like – from Greek statues to animals. Stick shapes together by pressing on gently. Put statues on greaseproof paper to dry out for 2 hours. Decorate the statues with edible coloured balls or paint on decorations with edible food colourings.

HOW TO PLAY 'GREEK STATUES'

First, you must make yourself look like an Ancient Greek. You can do this by wrapping yourself up in an old white sheet.

Next, dance around to some lively music. When the music stops you must freeze like a statue. If you move a muscle you drop out of the game.

The last person left standing as still as a statue wins the game.

HONEY AND LEMON CAKE ♟

100g (4oz) margarine
100g (4oz) caster sugar
2 eggs
150g (6oz) self-raising flour
2 × 5ml spoons (2 tsp) ground cinnamon
Grated rind of 1 lemon
25g (1oz) flaked almonds
2 × 15ml spoons (2 tbsp) clear honey

Set oven at 180°C (350°F), Gas Mark 4. Line an 18–20cm (7–8 inch) square cake tin with greaseproof paper. (Cut 2 lengths of paper the size of the base of the tin and long enough to extend up both sides of the tin.) Place inside the tin so that all the inside is covered with paper. Lightly grease with cooking oil.

Put margarine and sugar in a large mixing bowl. Cream together with a wooden spoon or electric mixer until pale and creamy.

Beat in one egg with one tablespoon of the measured flour until well mixed. Beat in the other egg with a tablespoon of flour. Adding the flour like this prevents the mixture from curdling.

Add remaining flour, cinnamon and lemon rind and fold in gently with a large metal spoon or spatula.

Spoon into the prepared tin and level the surface. Sprinkle the top with flaked almonds.

Bake in the pre-heated oven for 45 minutes until well risen, golden brown and firm to touch. Immediately spoon the honey on top and brush to the sides.

Leave to cool in the tin before lifting out with the greaseproof paper. Cut into 16 squares.

Lamb Kebabs can either be grilled or cooked on a barbecue for a fine day's party.

LAMB KEBABS ♟ Serves 4

Marinade:
2 × 15ml sp (2 tbsp) cooking oil
1 × 15ml sp (1 tbsp) lemon juice
1 × 15ml sp (1 tbsp) worcestershire sauce
1 × 15ml sp (1 tbsp) soft brown sugar
Kebabs:
450g (1lb) boned lamb (fillet/leg)
1 small green pepper
4 small tomatoes
4 button mushrooms

Mix together marinade ingredients. Cut meat in 2.5cm (1in) cubes. Put in a bowl. Pour over marinade. Cover and leave at room temperature for 2–4 hrs. Turn meat now and then.

Cut pepper in half. Remove core and seeds. Cut each half in 4. Arrange lamb on 4 skewers, alternating with pepper, tomatoes and mushrooms.

Put kebabs on grill pan. Pour over marinade. Cook under a moderately hot grill for about 15 mins. until all sides are browned. **Serve hot.**

Use oven gloves to turn skewers.

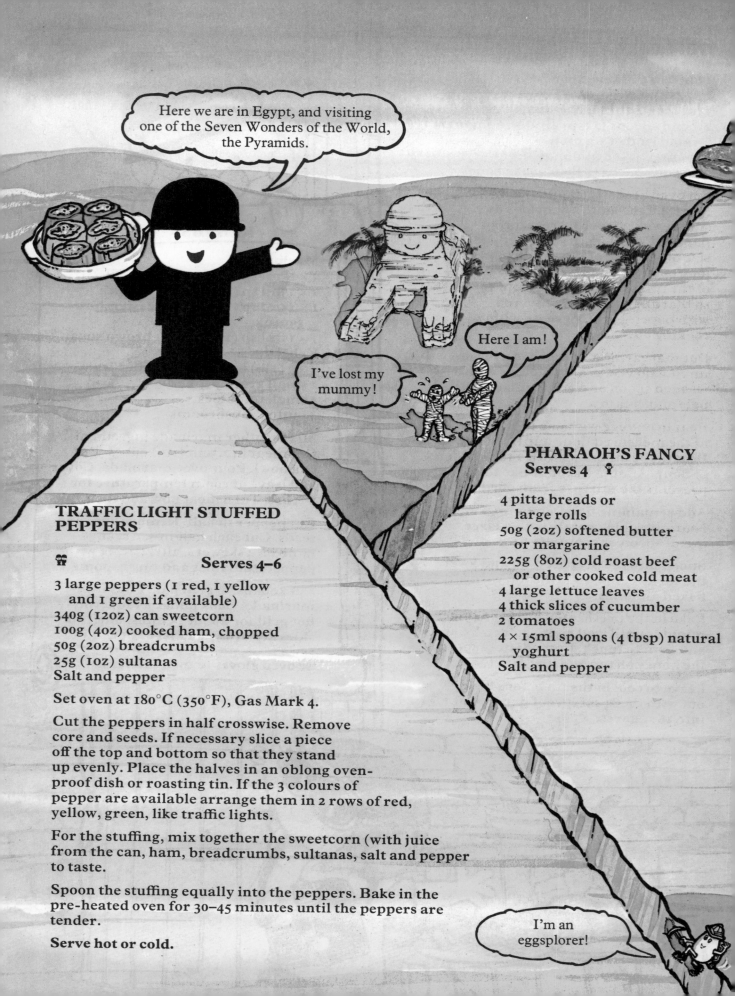

TRAFFIC LIGHT STUFFED PEPPERS

Serves 4–6

3 large peppers (1 red, 1 yellow
  and 1 green if available)
340g (12oz) can sweetcorn
100g (4oz) cooked ham, chopped
50g (2oz) breadcrumbs
25g (1oz) sultanas
Salt and pepper

Set oven at 180°C (350°F), Gas Mark 4.

Cut the peppers in half crosswise. Remove
core and seeds. If necessary slice a piece
off the top and bottom so that they stand
up evenly. Place the halves in an oblong ovenproof dish or roasting tin. If the 3 colours of
pepper are available arrange them in 2 rows of red,
yellow, green, like traffic lights.

For the stuffing, mix together the sweetcorn (with juice
from the can, ham, breadcrumbs, sultanas, salt and pepper
to taste.

Spoon the stuffing equally into the peppers. Bake in the
pre-heated oven for 30–45 minutes until the peppers are
tender.

Serve hot or cold.

PHARAOH'S FANCY
Serves 4

4 pitta breads or
  large rolls
50g (2oz) softened butter
  or margarine
225g (8oz) cold roast beef
  or other cooked cold meat
4 large lettuce leaves
4 thick slices of cucumber
2 tomatoes
4 × 15ml spoons (4 tbsp) natural
  yoghurt
Salt and pepper

The **Great Pyramid** was built almost five thousand years ago. It is made of more than 2,000,000 blocks of stone and probably took over 4,000 men more than 30 years to build. To re-build it today using modern equipment would still take 500 men 5 years.

PYRAMID PILAFF

225g (8oz) long grain rice
50g (2oz) sultanas
25g (1oz) walnuts
1 × 15ml spoon (1 tbsp) dried onion flakes
600ml (1 pint) water
1 chicken stock cube
1 × 2.5ml spoon ($\frac{1}{2}$ tsp) ground cinnamon
Pinch of salt and pepper
1 × 15ml spoon (1 tbsp) chopped parsley

Set oven at 190°C (375°F), Gas Mark 5. Put the rice in an ovenproof dish. Add sultanas, walnuts and dried onion and stir together until well mixed.

Boil the water in a kettle and pour 600ml (1 pint) into a measuring jug. Stir in stock cube, cinnamon, salt and pepper.

Pour hot stock over the rice. Cover the dish and cook in the pre-heated oven for 45 minutes until rice is cooked and all water has been absorbed.

Stir in chopped parsley with a fork. Shape into a mound like a pyramid. Serve hot with meat – it's especially good with **Lamb Kebabs, p. 13.**

This dish serves 4.

What to do:

With a round-bladed knife, cut the pittas along one side to make a pocket.

Cut the cold meat into long thin strips and place in a mixing bowl.

Cut the lettuce into long thin shreds and add to the bowl. Cut the cucumber slices into quarters and the tomato into wedges and add to the bowl.

Spoon over the yoghurt and add a pinch of salt and pepper. Stir until the filling is well mixed.

Spoon the filling equally into the 4 pockets of pitta bread.

We won't starve here in the desert. Thanks to all the sandwiches here!

And talking of sandwiches, those **Pharaoh's Fancies** are an appetising alternative for taking on picnics or for a salad lunch.

What's the difference between an old lettuce and an unhappy song?

One's a bad salad and the other's a sad ballad!

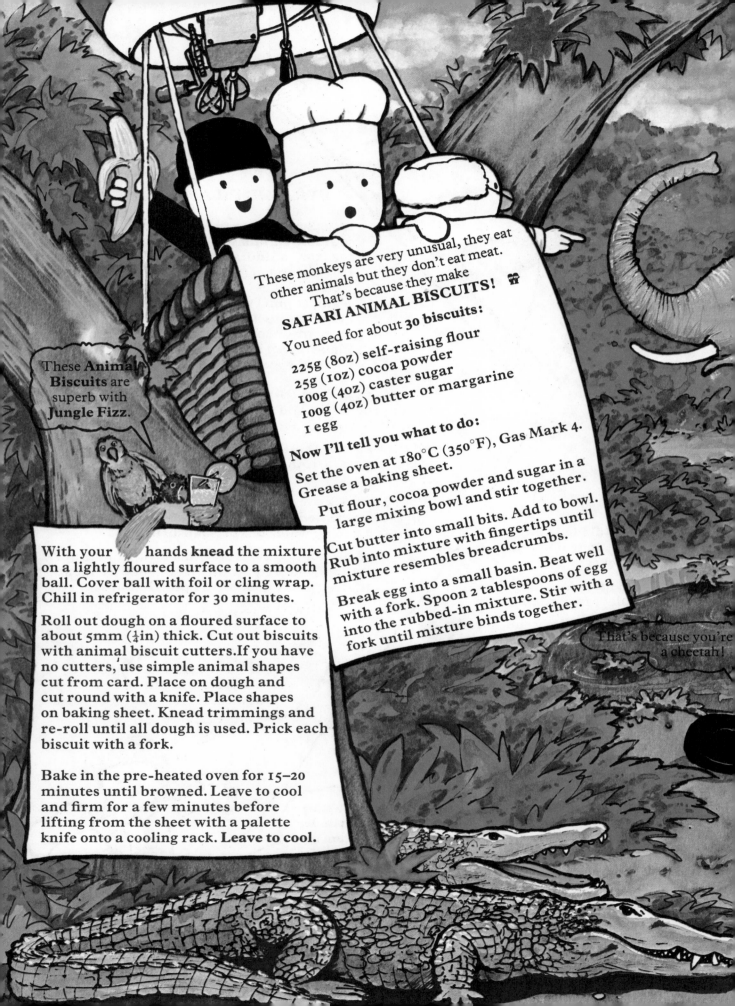

These monkeys are very unusual, they eat other animals but they don't eat meat. That's because they make

SAFARI ANIMAL BISCUITS!

You need for about **30 biscuits:**

225g (8oz) self-raising flour
25g (1oz) cocoa powder
100g (4oz) caster sugar
100g (4oz) butter or margarine
1 egg

Now I'll tell you what to do:

Set the oven at 180°C (350°F), Gas Mark 4. Grease a baking sheet.

Put flour, cocoa powder and sugar in a large mixing bowl and stir together.

Cut butter into small bits. Add to bowl. Rub into mixture with fingertips until mixture resembles breadcrumbs.

Break egg into a small basin. Beat well with a fork. Spoon 2 tablespoons of egg into the rubbed-in mixture. Stir with a fork until mixture binds together.

With your hands **knead** the mixture on a lightly floured surface to a smooth ball. Cover ball with foil or cling wrap. Chill in refrigerator for 30 minutes.

Roll out dough on a floured surface to about 5mm ($\frac{1}{4}$in) thick. Cut out biscuits with animal biscuit cutters. If you have no cutters, use simple animal shapes cut from card. Place on dough and cut round with a knife. Place shapes on baking sheet. Knead trimmings and re-roll until all dough is used. Prick each biscuit with a fork.

Bake in the pre-heated oven for 15–20 minutes until browned. Leave to cool and firm for a few minutes before lifting from the sheet with a palette knife onto a cooling rack. **Leave to cool.**

These **Animal Biscuits** are superb with **Jungle Fizz.**

That's because you're a cheetah!

I'm a sophisticated snake
who knows that if you take:

½ large cucumber or 1 small
  cucumber
300ml (½ pint) natural yoghurt
1 × 15ml spoon (1 tbsp) chopped
  fresh mint
OR 1 × 5ml spoon (1 tsp) dried mint
Pinch of salt and pepper

You can make a delicious
Indian side dish called
CUCUMBER RAITA.

This grade ♀ recipe is perfect with
Chicken Curry (see opposite page)
and this is what you do:

Cut cucumber into thin slices or
small cubes. Place in a bowl.

Mix yoghurt with chopped mint,
salt and pepper. Pour over the
cucumber and gently stir to mix well.

Transfer to a serving dish. Chill
in refrigerator until required.

This amount serves 4.

I'm a yogi
who loves yoghurt!

This Indian Cookbook
has a superb recipe for
SPICED VEGETABLES!

I'm a cur
who loves curries!

**INDIAN COOK BOOK
SPICED
VEGETABLES, ♀**
For 4 servings:
1 small onion
1 × 15ml spoon (1 tbsp)
  cooking oil
1 × 5ml spoon (1 tsp)
  curry powder
450g (1lb) cabbage
225g (8oz) spinach
150ml (¼ pint) water
1 × 15ml spoon (1 tbsp)
  lemon juice
Pinch of salt and pepper

Peel onion and cut in half. Place cut
sides down on chopping board. Chop
finely with a sharp knife.

Pour oil into large saucepan. Add
onion. Stir in curry powder with
wooden spoon. Cover pan and cook
over gentle heat for 5 minutes.

Remove any battered outside leaves
from cabbage. Cut off coarse stalk
at base. Shred leaves into small
pieces, with a sharp knife.

Remove stalks from spinach leaves.
Wash and drain cabbage and spinach.
Add to saucepan. Pour in water. Add
lemon juice, salt and pepper. Stir
gently to mix vegetables with spices.

Cover pan and bring to boil. Cook
over moderate heat for 5 minutes
until vegetables are just tender but
slightly crunchy and a bright colour.

Transfer to a warmed serving dish.
Serve at once.

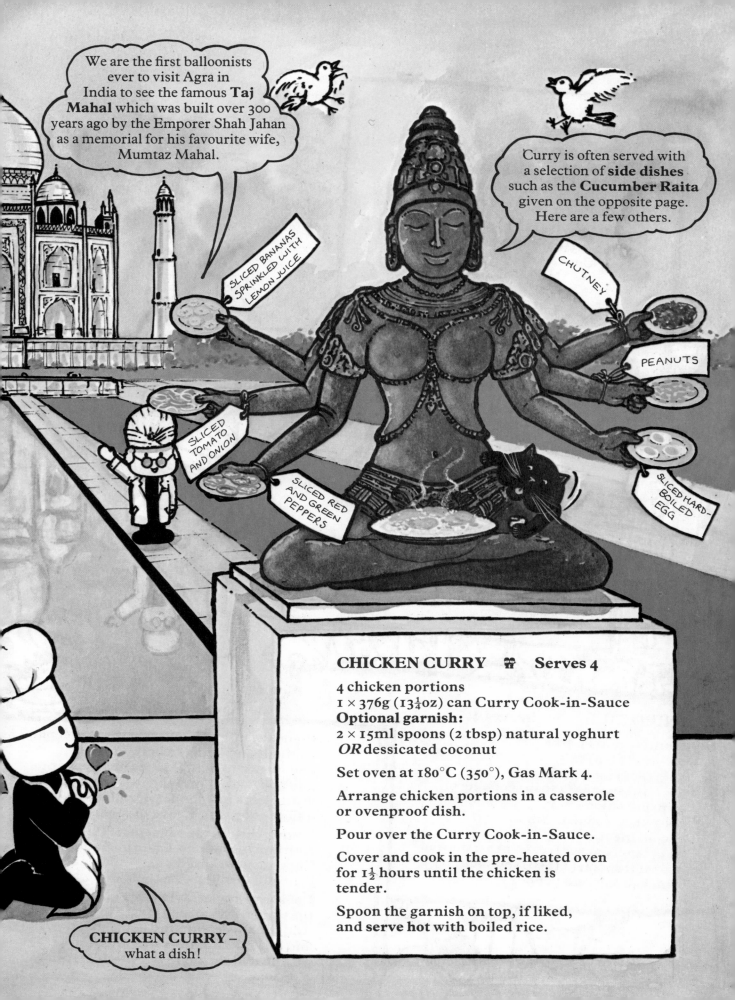

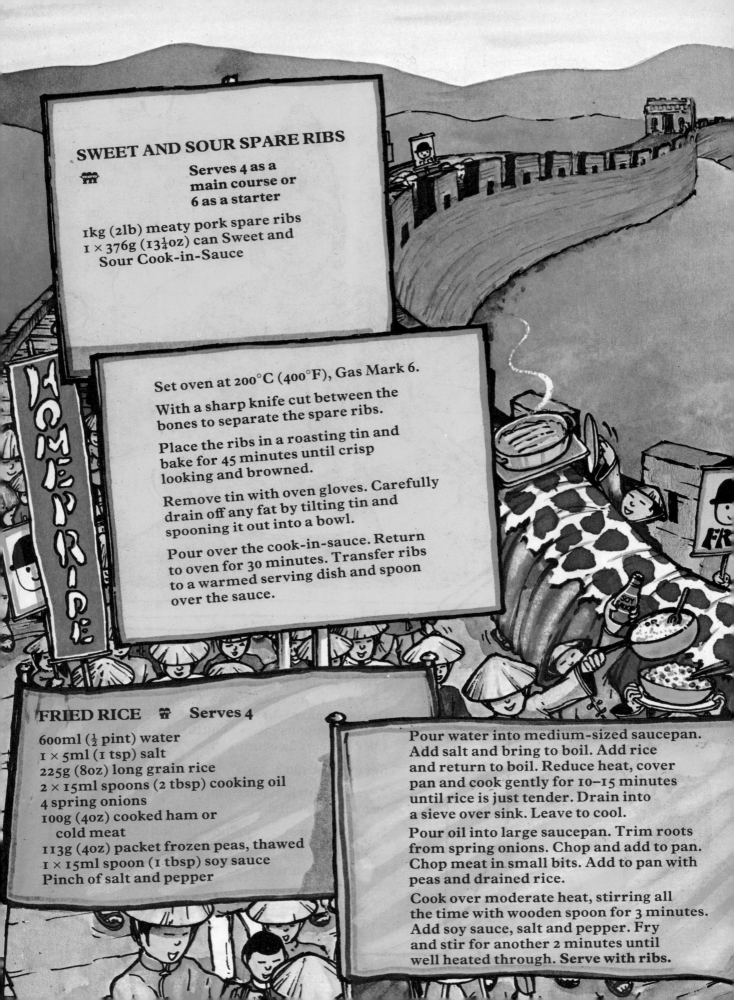

SWEET AND SOUR SPARE RIBS

Serves 4 as a
main course or
6 as a starter

1kg (2lb) meaty pork spare ribs
1 × 376g (13¼oz) can Sweet and
Sour Cook-in-Sauce

Set oven at 200°C (400°F), Gas Mark 6.

With a sharp knife cut between the
bones to separate the spare ribs.

Place the ribs in a roasting tin and
bake for 45 minutes until crisp
looking and browned.

Remove tin with oven gloves. Carefully
drain off any fat by tilting tin and
spooning it out into a bowl.

Pour over the cook-in-sauce. Return
to oven for 30 minutes. Transfer ribs
to a warmed serving dish and spoon
over the sauce.

FRIED RICE　　Serves 4

600ml (½ pint) water
1 × 5ml (1 tsp) salt
225g (8oz) long grain rice
2 × 15ml spoons (2 tbsp) cooking oil
4 spring onions
100g (4oz) cooked ham or
　　cold meat
113g (4oz) packet frozen peas, thawed
1 × 15ml spoon (1 tbsp) soy sauce
Pinch of salt and pepper

Pour water into medium-sized saucepan.
Add salt and bring to boil. Add rice
and return to boil. Reduce heat, cover
pan and cook gently for 10–15 minutes
until rice is just tender. Drain into
a sieve over sink. Leave to cool.

Pour oil into large saucepan. Trim roots
from spring onions. Chop and add to pan.
Chop meat in small bits. Add to pan with
peas and drained rice.

Cook over moderate heat, stirring all
the time with wooden spoon for 3 minutes.
Add soy sauce, salt and pepper. Fry
and stir for another 2 minutes until
well heated through. **Serve with ribs.**

Don't those recipes look delicious: **MANDARIN GATEAU, SWEET AND SOUR SPARE RIBS, and FRIED RICE!**

That's the **Great Wall of China.** It stretches for 3,460km and was built over two thousand years ago.

MANDARIN GATEAU

3 eggs
75g (3oz) caster sugar
75g (3oz) plain flour
Grated rind 1 small orange
100g (4oz) butter, softened
225g (8oz) icing sugar
1 × 15ml spoon (1 tbsp) orange juice
312g (11oz) can mandarin oranges, drained

Set oven at 190°C (375°F), Gas Mark 5. Prepare two 18–20cm (7–8in) sandwich tins. Cut 2 circles of greaseproof paper to fit inside base of tins. Brush inside tins with cooking oil, insert paper circle and brush this with oil, too.

Crack eggs in a large mixing bowl. Add sugar. Whisk with an electric mixer until very thick, pale and creamy. Add flour and orange rind. Fold gently in with a metal spoon until well mixed.

Did you say Fried Mice?!

Pour mixture equally into tins. Bake in pre-heated oven for 15–20 minutes until golden brown and firm at centre. Remove tins with oven gloves. Leave a few minutes and turn out on cooling rack. Peel off paper. Leave to cool.
To finish the cake. Place butter in a bowl. Beat until creamy. Beat in icing sugar then orange juice to give a spreading consistency. Place one layer of cake on plate. Spread top with half the cream. Reserve 12 good mandarins for top of cake. Spread rest over cream. Place 2nd layer on top, press on gently. Spread remaining butter cream on top and decorate around the edge with mandarins.

I am a **Red Kangaroo,** the biggest kangaroo there is! At 2.13m in height I am taller than almost any man and I can weigh up to 79kg.

Kangaroos are great jumpers. They can jump over 3.20m in height and can make a bound as great as 12.80m.

If you want to make **KANGAROO RAREBIT,** this is what you need for **4 servings:**

What do you get if you cross a sheep with a kangaroo?

A woolly jumper!

225g (8oz) cheddar cheese
4 × 15ml spoons (4 tbsp) tomato ketchup
Pinch of salt and pepper
4 slices of bread
4 rashers of bacon

And here's what you do:

Grate cheese and place in a mixing bowl. Add tomato ketchup, salt and pepper and stir until mixed.

Place slices of bread on a grill pan and grill until toasted. Turn over and lightly toast the other side.

Remove from grill. Divide cheese mixture between the 4 pieces of toast and spread to near the sides. Place a rasher of bacon across each slice and cook under a moderately hot grill for about 3 minutes until the cheese has melted and the bacon is crisp. Serve at once.

I really am a Kangaroo Rarebit! I am Australia's rarest marsupial: the **Sandhill Dunnart.**

Because we live on the other side of the world, people think we walk around upside down. We don't. But we do love **UPSIDE DOWN GINGER CAKE.** It's a grade 🐱 recipe.

To make it you need:

2 × 15ml spoons (2 tbsp) golden syrup
227g (8oz) can pineapple rings
7 glace cherries
100g (4oz) butter or margarine
100g (4oz) soft brown sugar
100g (4oz) golden syrup (or 4
   rounded tablespoons)
2 eggs
150ml (¼ pint) milk
225g (8oz) plain flour
   1 × 2.5ml spoon (½ tsp)
      bicarbonate of soda
   1 × 15ml spoon (1 tbsp)
      ground ginger

These are the instructions:

1. Set oven at 160°C (325°F), Gas Mark 3. Lightly grease a 20cm (8in) round cake tin.

2. Spoon syrup into tin and spread over base. Drain pineapple, put 1 ring in centre and cut remaining rings in half and arrange them round the edge of the base. Place a cherry in the centres of the rings.

3. Place butter, sugar and 4 tbsp of syrup in a small saucepan. Heat gently, stirring with a wooden spoon until butter and sugar dissolve. Remove from heat and leave to cool for about 15 minutes.

4. Crack eggs into a small basin. Beat well with a fork, then beat in milk. Stir egg and milk into cooled melted mixture.

5. Sift flour, soda and ginger into a large mixing bowl. Pour in melted mixture. Stir with a wooden spoon until well mixed. Pour into cake tin carefully over pineapple.

6. Bake in pre-heated oven for 1¼ hours until risen and firm to touch. Cool for a few minutes before turning out upside-down on a serving plate so that the pattern of pineapple will be on top. Serve hot as a pudding or cold as a cake.

THIS WAY U

MEXICO'S NUMBER

I'm going to make **CHILLI CON CARNE**, a grade 🎁 recipe. For 4 helpings I will need:

Miguel's Chilli is superb served hot with boiled rice and a salad.

450g (1lb) lean minced beef
1 green pepper
1 large stick celery
1 × 376g (13¼oz) can Chilli Cook-in-Sauce

What you do:

Put mince in a medium sized saucepan. Cut pepper in half. Remove all core and seeds. Cut pepper into small 1cm (½in) squares. Add to pan.

Wash celery. Cut across into slices. Add to pan. Stir in Chilli sauce.

Cover pan and bring to boil. Reduce heat to simmer gently for 20–30 mins. Stir now and then to prevent sticking.

PONCHO PUDDING 🎁 **Serves 4–6**

170g (6fl.oz) can evaporated milk
300ml (½ pint) water
135g (4¾oz) pkt. orange flavoured jelly tablet
2 × 15ml spoons (2 tbsp) instant coffee
1 chocolate flake bar.

Put milk in refrigerator to chill well.

Pour water into a small saucepan. Boil and remove from heat. Tear jelly tablet apart into small cubes. Add to hot water. Add coffee and stir it all until dissolved. Leave in cold place until just beginning to set (about 2½ hours).

When jelly is thick but not set, remove can of milk from refrigerator. pour into a large mixing bowl. Whisk until thick and foamy and the whisk leaves a trail. Whisk in the half-set jelly until well mixed. Pour into a serving bowl and chill in refrigerator until set.

Crumble over the chocolate flake to decorate.

Jose has made a delicious dessert called **PONCHO PUDDING.**

MEXICANA SALAD is a simple grade ♀ recipe. For a tasty salad for **4** or a succulent starter for **6** you will need:

350g (12oz) cooked chicken meat
150ml (¼ pint) mayonnaise
Few drops tabasco sauce (optional)
25g (1oz) walnuts, broken
1 avocado pear
1 × 15ml spoon (1 tbsp) lemon juice
Pinch of salt and pepper
1 small lettuce.

What you do:

Chop chicken into small pieces with a round bladed knife. Place in a bowl. Add mayonnaise, tabasco and walnuts and mix together.

Cut avocado in half. Remove stone and peel off skin. Cut avocado flesh into small cubes and add to chicken mixture.

Sprinkle with lemon juice immediately to prevent avocado from going brown. Add salt and pepper. Stir gently to mix so avocado is not mashed.

Wash and dry lettuce. Cut into shreds and place in base of serving dish or individual dishes. Pile chicken mixture on top. Chill until required.

Note: If avocado is unavailable, use 1 eating apple, cored and chopped, instead.

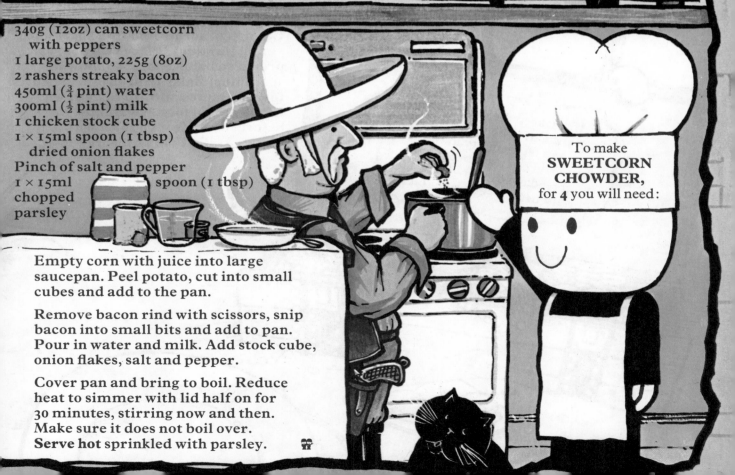

340g (12oz) can sweetcorn with peppers
1 large potato, 225g (8oz)
2 rashers streaky bacon
450ml (¾ pint) water
300ml (½ pint) milk
1 chicken stock cube
1 × 15ml spoon (1 tbsp) dried onion flakes
Pinch of salt and pepper
1 × 15ml spoon (1 tbsp) chopped parsley

To make **SWEETCORN CHOWDER**, for **4** you will need:

Empty corn with juice into large saucepan. Peel potato, cut into small cubes and add to the pan.

Remove bacon rind with scissors, snip bacon into small bits and add to pan. Pour in water and milk. Add stock cube, onion flakes, salt and pepper.

Cover pan and bring to boil. Reduce heat to simmer with lid half on for 30 minutes, stirring now and then. Make sure it does not boil over.
Serve hot sprinkled with parsley.

This Caribbean Island is full of surprises –
buried with a chest of treasure
I've found a recipe for
COCONUT REFRIGERATOR COOKIES, 💼

Here are the ingredients for about **32 cookies,**
but you needn't cook them all at once – the
biscuit dough can be kept in the refrigerator
for up to a week, and you can slice off the
number of biscuits you would like to bake and
return the remaining dough to the refrigerator.

100g (4oz) softened butter or margarine
100g (4oz) caster sugar
150g (6oz) plain flour
50g (2oz) dessicated coconut
1 × 5ml spoon (1 tsp) vanilla essence

Here's what you have to do:

Set oven at 190°C (375°F), Gas Mark 5.
Lightly grease a baking sheet.

Put butter and sugar in a large mixing bowl.
Cream together with a wooden spoon or
electric beater until pale and creamy.

Beat in flour, then beat in coconut and
vanilla essence until well mixed and crumbly.
Draw mixture together with your hands to
form a ball of dough.

On a lightly floured surface, roll into a
sausage with your hands about 20cm (8in) long.
Wrap in foil and chill in refrigerator for
about 1 hour until firm.

Cut dough across into thin slices about
5mm (¼in) thick. Place well apart on
prepared baking sheet to allow for
spreading. Bake in the pre-heated oven
for 10 minutes until golden brown.
Leave to cool for a few minutes
before lifting from a sheet with a
palette knife. Cool on a wire rack.

If you keep the melon seeds
from the **Caribbean Fruit Salad**
and let them dry in the
sun you can use a needle and
thread to string together a
pretty **melon seed necklace.**

I'm just picking some bananas for this tasty **BANANA TEABREAD,** These are the ingredients I will need:

225g (8oz) self-raising flour
100g (4oz) butter or margarine
100g (4oz) caster sugar
100g (4oz) sultanas
3 medium bananas, about
    450g (1lb)
2 eggs

Set oven at 180°C (350°F), Gas Mark 4. Lightly grease a 1kg (2lb) loaf tin.

Put the flour in a large mixing bowl. Add butter cut up in small bits. Rub butter into flour with finger-tips until mixture resembles fine bread-crumbs. Stir in sugar and sultanas.

Peel bananas and mash well with a fork. Add to bowl.

Crack eggs in a small basin. Beat with a fork. Pour into the mixture and stir until well mixed. Pour into prepared loaf tin.

Bake in the pre-heated oven for 1 hour until golden brown and risen. To test if teabread is done, insert a skewer into the middle. It should come out clean. Leave to cool in the tin before turning out.

To make **CARIBBEAN FRUIT SALAD,** for **4** you need a Honeydew melon like this. **Here are all the ingredients:**

1 medium sized ripe Honeydew melon, about
    1kg (2lb)
439g (15½oz) can pineapple pieces
2 × 15ml spoons (2 tbsp) soft dark brown sugar
2 glace cherries

Cut melon in half crosswise. Scoop out seeds with a spoon. Scoop melon out in small pieces with a teaspoon – place in a mixing bowl. Drain pineapple and add pieces to melon. Pile back into melon shells. Sprinkle brown sugar on each half and top with a cherry. Chill until required.

he world's largest ater melon weighed .8kg.

BOSTON BROWNIES 👥 Makes 16 squares

75g (3oz) butter or margarine
50g (2oz) plain chocolate
150g (6oz) dark soft brown sugar
75g (3oz) self-raising flour
1 × 2.5ml spoon (½ tsp) vanilla essence
2 eggs
50g (2oz) walnuts, roughly chopped

Set oven at 180°C (350°F), Gas Mark 4. Lightly grease a 20cm (8in) square shallow cake tin.

Place butter in medium sized saucepan. Add chocolate broken into small bits. Heat gently stirring with a wooden spoon until melted. Remove from heat and stir in the sugar until dissolved.

Crack eggs into a small basin. Add vanilla essence and beat with a fork.

Pour beaten eggs into the saucepan. Add the flour. Beat with a wooden spoon until well mixed. Stir in the walnuts. Pour mixture into prepared tin.

Bake in a pre-heated oven for 40–45 minutes until risen and firm to touch but slightly soft inside and the surface will be cracked.

Cool before cutting into squares.

> We've arrived in the U.S.A. These New Yorkers seem pleased to see us.

> Yes, they're preparing some favourite American dishes for us, too!

SKYSCRAPER GLORY 🍦

1 × 483ml block icecream
1 × 397g (14oz) can cherry fruit pie filling
4 wafers or tall biscuits

Remove the ice cream from freezer, 5 minutes before using to soften slightly. Spoon a layer of ice cream into the base of 4 tall serving glasses.

Spoon a layer of cherry filling on top of the ice cream, then another layer of ice cream and continue layers until all the cherry filling and ice cream are used.

Stick a wafer in the top and serve at once.

Note: Any flavour of fruit filling can be used instead of the cherry.

Serves 4

> There is the **Empire State building.** For many years it was the tallest building in the world, but now the tallest building is not in New York at all. It is in another American city, Chicago, where the Sears tower rises to 443m with 110 storeys, 103 lifts and 16,000 windows!

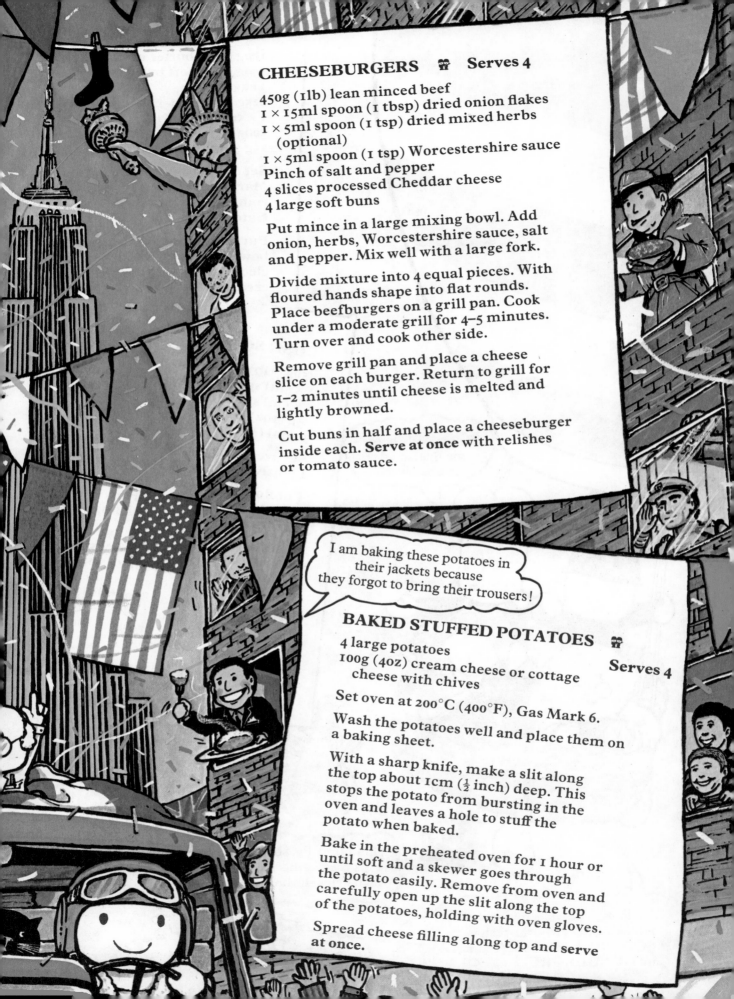

CHEESEBURGERS 👥👥 Serves 4

450g (1lb) lean minced beef
1 × 15ml spoon (1 tbsp) dried onion flakes
1 × 5ml spoon (1 tsp) dried mixed herbs
   (optional)
1 × 5ml spoon (1 tsp) Worcestershire sauce
Pinch of salt and pepper
4 slices processed Cheddar cheese
4 large soft buns

Put mince in a large mixing bowl. Add onion, herbs, Worcestershire sauce, salt and pepper. Mix well with a large fork.

Divide mixture into 4 equal pieces. With floured hands shape into flat rounds. Place beefburgers on a grill pan. Cook under a moderate grill for 4–5 minutes. Turn over and cook other side.

Remove grill pan and place a cheese slice on each burger. Return to grill for 1–2 minutes until cheese is melted and lightly browned.

Cut buns in half and place a cheeseburger inside each. **Serve at once** with relishes or tomato sauce.

I am baking these potatoes in their jackets because they forgot to bring their trousers!

BAKED STUFFED POTATOES 👥👥 Serves 4

4 large potatoes
100g (4oz) cream cheese or cottage cheese with chives

Set oven at 200°C (400°F), Gas Mark 6.

Wash the potatoes well and place them on a baking sheet.

With a sharp knife, make a slit along the top about 1cm ($\frac{1}{2}$ inch) deep. This stops the potato from bursting in the oven and leaves a hole to stuff the potato when baked.

Bake in the preheated oven for 1 hour or until soft and a skewer goes through the potato easily. Remove from oven and carefully open up the slit along the top of the potatoes, holding with oven gloves.

Spread cheese filling along top and serve at once.

DUNDEE FRUIT CAKE 👥

150g (6oz) butter or margarine
150g (6oz) soft brown sugar
3 eggs
225g (8oz) self-raising flour
1 × 5ml spoon (1 tsp) mixed spice
500g (1.1lb) pkt. mixed dried fruit
25g (1oz) split almonds

Set oven at 160°C (325°F) Gas Mark 3. Prepare a 20cm (8in) round cake tin as for **Mandarin Gateau, page 21.**

Put butter and sugar in a large bowl. Beat with wooden spoon or electric mixer until pale and creamy.

IRISH SODA BREAD 👥

450g (1lb) plain flour
1 × 5ml spoon (1 tsp) bicarbonate of soda
1 × 5ml spoon (1 tsp) cream of tartar
25g (1oz) lard
300ml (½ pint) milk

Set oven at 200°C (400°F) Gas Mark 6. Lightly grease a baking tray.

Put flour in a large mixing bowl. Stir in soda and cream of tartar. Add lard in small bits. Rub in with fingertips.

Make a well in centre of flour. Pour in milk. Stir in with wooden spoon to a soft dough. Knead dough with your hand on a lightly floured surface to a smooth ball. Shape into an 18cm (7in) round and place on baking sheet. With a sharp knife score a cross on the top about 1cm (½in) deep.

Bake in oven for 30 minutes until well risen and browned. Leave to cool on a wire rack.

Beat in eggs, one at a time, with a rounded tablespoon of the flour. Beat well.

Fold in remaining flour, spice and dried fruit with a metal spoon. Spoon mixture into cake tin and level top. Arrange almond halves, rounded sides up on top of cake. Press on gently.

Bake in a pre-heated oven for 2 hours until golden-brown and firm to touch. When cake is done a skewer inserted in the centre will come out clean. Leave to cool in tin before turning out.

TREACLE TART

150g (6oz) plain flour
Pinch of salt
40g (1½oz) margarine
40g (1½oz) lard
2 × 15ml spoons cold water
100g (4oz) breadcrumbs
6 × 15ml spoons (6 tbsp) golden syrup
½ a lemon

Set oven at 190°C (375°F), Gas Mark 5.

Put flour and salt in a mixing bowl. Cut margarine and lard in small bits and add to flour. Rub in with fingertips until mixture resembles fine breadcrumbs. Sprinkle in the water. Use a round-bladed knife to mix to a firm dough.

Place on a lightly floured surface. Knead gently with fingertips to a smooth ball of dough. Roll out pastry with a lightly floured rolling pin to a 23cm (9in) circle. Lift onto an ovenproof pie plate. Trim overlapping edges.

Put breadcrumbs in a bowl. Add syrup. Finely grate rind from half a lemon into bowl. Squeeze juice from the half and add to bowl. Mix filling together. Spread over base leaving a pastry rim.

Bake in pre-heated oven for 30 minutes until pastry is golden brown round edge and filling is golden.

Dundee Fruit Cake is best stored in an airtight container.

Treacle Tart is a delight, hot or cold.

You can test if the bread is ready by lifting it off the baking sheet with oven gloves and tapping underneath with your knuckles.

If the bread is cooked it will sound hollow.

For a fancier tart, cut any pastry trimmings into narrow strips and place them on top of the filling in a criss-cross pattern, pressing ends gently onto the rim of pastry, before baking.

USEFUL COOKERY TERMS

Beat or Cream – to mix ingredients together until light, or beat air into a mixture. Use a wooden spoon or electric beater.

Bind – to add sufficient liquid to dry ingredients to hold the mixture together.

Glaze – to brush a liquid such as beaten egg, milk, syrup on sweet or savoury foods, e.g. bread, pastry, to give a shiny surface.

Fold in – used to combine ingredients gently without losing any air in the mixture, e.g. whisked egg whites or cake mixtures. Use a large metal spoon or spatula.

Knead – to work dough or pastry with the hands to the consistency described in the recipe to form a smooth surface. Pastry should be kneaded very gently, whereas bread requires strong kneading.

Rub in – used to mix fat into dry ingredients using the fingertips until the mixture resembles breadcrumbs, e.g. for pastry, some cakes and biscuits. Pick up handfuls of the mixture in a bowl and rub between your thumb and fingertips allowing the ingredients to fall back into the bowl. Continue until evenly blended.

Sieve or Sift – to rub ingredients through a sieve with a wooden spoon to remove lumps and incorporate air.

Simmer – to boil very slowly so that there are only occasional small bubbles on the surface – it should never bubble rapidly.

Whisk or Whip – to beat air into a mixture with an electric mixer or hand-held whisk until thick and light and foamy, e.g. egg whites, cream. Whisked ingredients are always folded into other ingredients.

If you are still in doubt, ask an adult to show you what to do.

The terms above are commonly used in this and other recipe books. I've explained them for you in case you are not familiar with some of the techniques.